PROFESSIONAL RESOURCES

The Four-Blocks™ Literacy Model

Making Words: Lessons for Home or School Grade 1

by

Patricia M. Cunningham

and

Dorothy P. Hall

Editors	Cover Design
Joey Bland	Julie Webb
Tracy Soles	

D1295304

ISBN 0-88724-660-5

Table of Contents

Introduction

For most teachers, deciding what to give children for homework is a constant concern, similar in many ways to the daily task of deciding what to cook for dinner! When deciding what to cook for dinner, we have to choose foods that will not only fill everyone up, but also have nutritional value. In deciding what homework to give students, we have to make sure that the assignment does not just fill time, but also provides practice with important skills. Planning dinner for several people is complicated by the facts that people don't all like the same foods, and different people have different nutritional needs. Planning homework assignments is complicated by the different ability levels of the children—what some children need to practice, others have already mastered, and still others are not ready for.

Making Words is used in many classrooms, and most children view it as a "game-like, puzzle-solving" activity. They enjoy manipulating the letters and are intrigued with the idea that changing just one letter in the word or changing the order of the letters can create a totally different word. They like trying to figure out the secret word and sorting the words they made by spelling patterns. Most children also view figuring out the transfer words based on the sorted rhyming words as a "puzzle to be solved." Teachers like doing Making Words with their students because the students are actually engaged in a "hands-on, minds-on" activity through which they can discover how the English spelling system works and how letters are combined to decode and spell words. Teachers also appreciate the fact that Making Words is a multilevel activity—there is something in each lesson for every level of learner.

Having watched the success of Making Words activities with thousands of teachers and children, and being aware of how difficult it is to come up with good, meaningful, multilevel homework assignments, we began talking about how great it would be to come up with a Making Words lesson format which students could do with the help of an older child or tutor at school, or at home with a parent. As we began, we had many questions. How would the child know which words to make? How would the sort and transfer steps work? When we remembered that the parents of most young children are willing to help with homework if they know what to do and if the homework has a puzzle or game-like quality, it was easy to design the format. Here is how the Student Lesson Sheet format works, along with some suggestions for "selling" it to your students' parents.

The Student Lesson Sheet Format

Each lesson sheet has the letters needed across the top. The first thing children should do is to turn the paper over and write the capital letters on the back. This will give students the capital letters they will need if they are making a name. (If the lesson sheet is assigned as homework, it is a good idea to have the students turn their sheets over and write these capital letters before they leave your classroom.) When children begin their assignment, they will cut the letters apart and use these to make the words.

The area on the left side of the sheet has lines for writing the words after the children have made them. The small lines indicate the number of letters needed to spell each word. Children should make the words with their cut-apart letters and then write the letters on the appropriate lines. Because writing is difficult and arduous for many young children, helpers should be encouraged

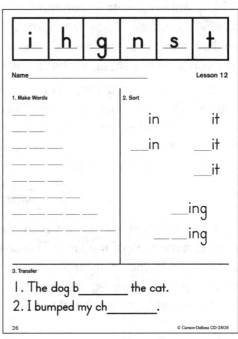

to help children write the words on the lines, perhaps even taking turns writing the words with the child.

The area on the right side of the sheet has the rhyming patterns for which the children will be sorting. The pattern (vowel to the end of the word) is already printed. The child's job is to finish the words by adding the beginning letters.

At the bottom of each sheet, there are two sentences with a missing word in each. The missing word is the transfer word, and it uses one of the rhyming patterns from the right side of the sheet. The beginning letters are provided, and the children must choose the correct rhyming pattern to make a word which begins with those letters and makes sense in the sentence.

Communicating with Making Words Helpers

We spent a lot of time thinking about how to communicate to the Making Words helpers what they need to do. After much discussion, we decided to put general directions and the list of words for five lessons in each helper letter. Staple this letter closed or put it in a sealed envelope, and make sure that helpers and children understand that it is not to be opened except by the Making Words helper! (This letter should be sent home with the students <u>first</u>, followed by one or two lessons per week.)

We tried to keep the directions for helpers very simple, while still providing hints they could give the child to make the activity as worthwhile and successful as possible. Because we know that some children will be doing this assignment at school with a tutor or at home with someone other than a parent—grandparent, older sibling, baby-sitter, or others, we addressed the letter to the "Making Words Helper."

If possible, complete one lesson with parents at a parent night or open house. Take them through the lesson, having them pretend to be students and complete each step. Have them write the capital letters on the back, cut the letters apart, make and write the words, and complete the rhyming words and sentences. Use the kinds of clues with the parents that you want them to use with their children, for example:

Change just the first letter to spell….

Add just one letter and spell….

If you move the letters in this word around, these same letters can spell a different word.

I'll give you a minute to guess the secret word, and then I'll give you some clues.

Try to communicate to parents that Making Words should be a fun and worthwhile activity. Children love solving the puzzle of how letters make words. Through this hands-on discovery process, they become good spellers and word decoders. Encourage parents to help children as they need help, particularly with writing the words on the sheet, so that the writing does not take away from the fun of the activity.

Finally, we know that if a lesson is assigned as homework, a small minority of parents can't or won't do this activity with their child. If some children don't have a Making Words helper at home, perhaps you could enlist the help of an older child at your school who could complete this activity with a younger student before or after school. In this way, even those children without a Making Words helper at home could still learn from the activity and participate in the checking of the assignment.

Checking the Making Words Lesson Sheet

Children should check their own Making Words Lesson sheets, and the lessons should be completely correct almost all of the time. The easiest and fastest way to check the lesson is to make a transparency copy of it. Put the transparency on an overhead projector, and let the children tell you what they wrote on their papers as you write the answers on the transparency. Be sure to "brag" on students' success by telling them what good spellers and word decoders they are becoming!

Dear Making Words Helper,

Making Words is an activity which helps children become good spellers and word decoders. The attached Making Words lesson is like a puzzle for students to solve with your help. Children enjoy cutting out the letters and arranging them to see that by changing just one letter, adding one letter, or moving the letters around, they have a whole new word. Children also enjoy the puzzle of figuring out the secret word which can be made from all the letters in the activity. (Hide the bottom section of this sheet so that you can keep the **bolded** secret words a secret!)

Your child does Making Words lessons in class, so he or she should be familiar with the steps of making the words, sorting them into rhyming patterns (such as all the words that end in **an**, **ash**, etc.), and then reading and spelling some different words that use the same rhyming patterns. Here are the steps that are needed for each lesson:

1. Help the child write the capital letters on the backs of the letter cards (if they did not complete this while in class), and then cut the letters apart.
2. Use the word list below to identify the words for each lesson. You will need to tell the child what words to spell from their letters. Some sample hints and sentences you might give for a Making Words lesson are listed below. This example is for Lesson 5, which includes a name and two words that can be made with the same letters. Have the child use the letter cards to make the words, then help him or her write the words on the lesson sheet as you work through the lesson. You might say:
   - Use 2 letters to spell **at**. (We are **at** home.)
   - Take the **t** away and add a letter to spell **an**. (**An** elephant is very big.)
   - Add a letter to **an** to spell **ant**. (The **ant** crawled up my arm.)
   - Use the same letters you used for **ant** but move them around to make them spell **tan**. (**Tan** is a light brown color.)
   - Now, let's spell another 3-letter word, **hat**. (His **hat** blew off in the wind.)
   - Let's spell a name. Use four letters to spell **Hank**. Don't forget that names need capital letters.
   - Change just the first letter and you can spell **tank**. (We pump gas into the gas **tank**.)
   - It's time for the secret word. Leave the letters in **tank** where they are, but add the **h** in somewhere, and you will have it. (Give the child a minute and then give clues.) This is a word you say when someone gives you something. It begins with **th**. **Thank** you.
3. Using the words made as reference, help the child to complete the sort section of the worksheet by adding the correct beginning letter(s) to the spelling patterns. If the pattern is a word, that word is provided. Read the rhyming words together.
4. Help the child read the sentences listed at the bottom of the lesson sheet and use the rhyming pattern(s) to spell a new word that makes sense in each sentence.

✂ —

Words for Lessons 1-5
(The *l* indicates words that can be made with the same letters.)

Lesson 1	an at pat pal pan tan plan **plant**
Lesson 2	an at cat can tan/ant than **chant**
Lesson 3	as am Sam ham has/ash mash **smash**
Lesson 4	an as ask can cans/scan sack **snack**
Lesson 5	at an ant/tan hat Hank tank **thank**

Dear Making Words Helper,

Making Words is an activity which helps children become good spellers and word decoders. The attached Making Words lesson is like a puzzle for students to solve with your help. Children enjoy cutting out the letters and arranging them to see that by changing just one letter, adding one letter, or moving the letters around, they have a whole new word. Children also enjoy the puzzle of figuring out the secret word which can be made from all the letters in the activity. (Hide the bottom section of this sheet so that you can keep the **bolded** secret words a secret!)

Your child does Making Words lessons in class, so he or she should be familiar with the steps of making the words, sorting them into rhyming patterns (such as all the words that end in **an**, **ash**, etc.), and then reading and spelling some different words that use the same rhyming patterns. Here are the steps that are needed for each lesson:

1. Help the child write the capital letters on the backs of the letter cards (if they did not complete this while in class), and then cut the letters apart.

2. Use the word list below to identify the words for each lesson. You will need to tell the child what words to spell from their letters. Some sample hints and sentences you might give for a Making Words lesson are listed below. This example is for Lesson 6. Have the child use the letter cards to make the words, then help him or her write the words on the lesson sheet as you work through the lesson. You might say:

   - Use 3 letters to spell **ham**. (Do you like to eat **ham**?)
   - Change the first letter to spell the name **Sam**. Remember that names begin with a capital letter.
   - Change the first letter to spell another name, **Pam**.
   - Use the same letters you used for **Pam** but move them around to make them spell **map**. (A **map** helps us find places.)
   - Change the first letter and spell **cap**. (Do you wear a **cap** on your head?)
   - Add one letter to **cap** to spell **camp**. (We like to **camp** out and sleep in tents.)
   - Add one letter to **camp** and you can spell **champ**. (We call the winner a **champ**.)
   - It's time for the secret word. Leave the letters in **champ** where they are, but add the **s** in somewhere and you will have it. (Give the child a minute and then give clues.) This is the word you use when you have more than one **champ**. We are the **champs**!

3. Using the words made as reference, help the child to complete the sort section of the worksheet by adding the correct beginning letter(s) to the spelling patterns. If the pattern is a word, that word is provided. Read the rhyming words together.

4. Help the child read the sentences listed at the bottom of the lesson sheet and use the rhyming pattern(s) to spell a new word that makes sense in each sentence.

✂ –

Words for Lessons 6-10

(The / indicates words that can be made with the same letters.)

Lesson 6	ham Sam Pam/map cap camp champ **champs**
Lesson 7	as ask ark has/ash rash shark **sharks**
Lesson 8	at sat rat war was/saw raw **straw**
Lesson 9	as at all sat salt/last tall **stall**
Lesson 10	it in pin pit/tip rip trip **print**

Dear Making Words Helper,

Making Words is an activity which helps children become good spellers and word decoders. The attached Making Words lesson is like a puzzle for students to solve with your help. Children enjoy cutting out the letters and arranging them to see that by changing just one letter, adding one letter, or moving the letters around, they have a whole new word. Children also enjoy the puzzle of figuring out the secret word which can be made from all the letters in the activity. (Hide the bottom section of this sheet so that you can keep the **bolded** secret words a secret!)

Your child does Making Words lessons in class, so he or she should be familiar with the steps of making the words, sorting them into rhyming patterns (such as all the words that end in **an**, **ash**, etc.), and then reading and spelling some different words that use the same rhyming patterns. Here are the steps that are needed for each lesson:

1. Help the child write the capital letters on the backs of the letter cards (if they did not complete this while in class), and then cut the letters apart.
2. Use the word list below to identify the words for each lesson. You will need to tell the child what words to spell from their letters. Some sample hints and sentences you might give for a Making Words lesson are listed below. This example is for Lesson 13, which has two secret words. Have the child use the letter cards to make the words, then help him or her write the words on the lesson sheet as you work through the lesson. You might say:
   - Use 2 letters to spell **is**. (Making words **is** fun.)
   - Use 3 letters to spell **sip**. (Take a little **sip** and make sure that drink is not too hot.)
   - Change the first letter to spell **lip**. (I bit my **lip**.)
   - Add a letter to **lip** and you can spell **lips**. (I have two **lips**.)
   - Move the letters in **lips** around and spell **slip**. (Be careful you don't **slip** on the ice.)
   - Use four letters to spell **pill**. (It is time to take your **pill**.)
   - This lesson has two secret words. Leave the letters in **pill** where they are but add the **s** in two different places and see what two words you can make. (Give the child a minute and then give clues.) Put the **s** on the end and what do you have? Be careful you don't **spill** the **pills**.
3. Using the words made as reference, help the child to complete the sort section of the worksheet by adding the correct beginning letter(s) to the spelling patterns. If the pattern is a word, that word is provided. Read the rhyming words together.
4. Help the child read the sentences listed at the bottom of the lesson sheet and use the rhyming pattern(s) to spell a new word that makes sense in each sentence.

✂ - ✂ - - - - -

Words for Lessons 11-15

(The / indicates words that can be made with the same letters.)

Lesson 11   in it hit kit ink tin thin **think**
Lesson 12   it in tin hit sit sing thing **things**
Lesson 13   is sip lip lips/slip pill **spill/pills** (2 secret words)
Lesson 14   hi it pit hit hip chip itch **pitch**
Lesson 15   Ed bed Ned/end ends/send bend **bends**

Dear Making Words Helper,

Making Words is an activity which helps children become good spellers and word decoders. The attached Making Words lesson is like a puzzle for students to solve with your help. Children enjoy cutting out the letters and arranging them to see that by changing just one letter, adding one letter, or moving the letters around, they have a whole new word. Children also enjoy the puzzle of figuring out the secret word which can be made from all the letters in the activity. (Hide the bottom section of this sheet so that you can keep the **bolded** secret words a secret!)

Your child does Making Words lessons in class, so he or she should be familiar with the steps of making the words, sorting them into rhyming patterns (such as all the words that end in **an**, **ash**, etc.), and then reading and spelling some different words that use the same rhyming patterns. Here are the steps that are needed for each lesson:

1. Help the child write the capital letters on the backs of the letter cards (if they did not complete this while in class), and then cut the letters apart.

2. Use the word list below to identify the words for each lesson. You will need to tell the child what words to spell from their letters. Some sample hints and sentences you might give for a Making Words lesson are listed below. This example is for Lesson 17, which has two secret words. Have the child use the letter cards to make the words, then help him or her write the words on the lesson sheet as you work through the lesson. You might say:

   • Use 2 letters to spell **us**. (She told **us** to come at 8:00.)
   • Add 1 letter to spell **bus**. (Some people ride the **bus** to work.)
   • Move the letters in **bus** around to spell **sub**. (When the teacher is sick, we have a **sub**.)
   • Change 1 letter and spell **hub**. (The **hub** is the center of something. We have **hub**caps on our wheels.)
   • Change the first letter and spell **rub**. (I would like to have a back **rub**.)
   • Use 4 letters to spell **rush**. (We had to **rush** home to watch our favorite program.)
   • There are two secret words today. Leave the letters in **rush** where they are but add the **b** somewhere and you will have one of them. The other one is harder. (Give the child a minute and then give sentence clues for the two words.) My dog likes me to **brush** him. A small bush is called a **shrub**.

3. Using the words made as reference, help the child to complete the sort section of the worksheet by adding the correct beginning letter(s) to the spelling patterns. If the pattern is a word, that word is provided. Read the rhyming words together.

4. Help the child read the sentences listed at the bottom of the lesson sheet and use the rhyming pattern(s) to spell a new word that makes sense in each sentence.

✂ — ✂ — — — — —

Words for Lessons 16-20

(The / indicates words that can be made with the same letters.)

Lesson 16   us rug hug hugs/gush rush rugs **shrug**
Lesson 17   us bus/sub hub rub rush **brush/shrub** (2 secret words)
Lesson 18   to so rot hot shot rots/sort **short**
Lesson 19   in an ran ban bar bran rain **brain**
Lesson 20   an at rat/art tan ran rain **train**

Dear Making Words Helper,

Making Words is an activity which helps children become good spellers and word decoders. The attached Making Words lesson is like a puzzle for students to solve with your help. Children enjoy cutting out the letters and arranging them to see that by changing just one letter, adding one letter, or moving the letters around, they have a whole new word. Children also enjoy the puzzle of figuring out the secret word which can be made from all the letters in the activity. (Hide the bottom section of this sheet so that you can keep the **bolded** secret words a secret!)

Your child does Making Words lessons in class, so he or she should be familiar with the steps of making the words, sorting them into rhyming patterns (such as all the words that end in **an**, **ash**, etc.), and then reading and spelling some different words that use the same rhyming patterns. Here are the steps that are needed for each lesson:

1. Help the child write the capital letters on the backs of the letter cards (if they did not complete this while in class), and then cut the letters apart.

2. Use the word list below to identify the words for each lesson. You will need to tell the child what words to spell from their letters. Some sample hints and sentences you might give for a Making Words lesson are listed below. This example is for Lesson 23, which has two secret words. Have the child use the letter cards to make the words, then help him or her write the words on the lesson sheet as you work through the lesson. You might say:

    *   Use 2 letters to spell **at**. (The movie starts **at** 7:00.)
    *   Add 1 letter to spell **rat**. (A cat will chase a **rat**.)
    *   Change 1 letter to spell **sat**. (We **sat** in the front row.)
    *   Change the last letter and spell **say**. (What did you **say**?)
    *   Change the first letter and spell the name **Ray**. Remember to use a capital letter.
    *   Turn the **R** over, add one letter, and spell **tray**. (Put your food on your **tray**.)
    *   There are two secret words today. Leave the letters in **tray** where they are and add the **s** in two different places to spell two words. (Give the child a minute and then give sentence clues for the two words.) Can you pick up all the **trays**? We adopted a **stray** dog.

3. Using the words made as reference, help the child to complete the sort section of the worksheet by adding the correct beginning letter(s) to the spelling patterns. If the pattern is a word, that word is provided. Read the rhyming words together.

4. Help the child read the sentences listed at the bottom of the lesson sheet and use the rhyming pattern(s) to spell a new word that makes sense in each sentence.

✂ —

Words for Lessons 21-25

(The / indicates words that can be made with the same letters.)

Lesson 21 at ate/eat sat set seat Kate **skate**
Lesson 22 at ate/eat Pat pet let late **plate**
Lesson 23 at rat sat say Ray tray **trays/stray** (2 secret words)
Lesson 24 Al pal/lap yap/pay lay play **plays**
Lesson 25 me met set seat meat/team **teams/steam** (2 secret words)

Dear Making Words Helper,

Making Words is an activity which helps children become good spellers and word decoders. The attached Making Words lesson is like a puzzle for students to solve with your help. Children enjoy cutting out the letters and arranging them to see that by changing just one letter, adding one letter, or moving the letters around, they have a whole new word. Children also enjoy the puzzle of figuring out the secret word which can be made from all the letters in the activity. (Hide the bottom section of this sheet so that you can keep the **bolded** secret words a secret!)

Your child does Making Words lessons in class, so he or she should be familiar with the steps of making the words, sorting them into rhyming patterns (such as all the words that end in **an**, **ash**, etc.), and then reading and spelling some different words that use the same rhyming patterns. Here are the steps that are needed for each lesson:

1. Help the child write the capital letters on the backs of the letter cards (if they did not complete this while in class), and then cut the letters apart.

2. Use the word list below to identify the words for each lesson. You will need to tell the child what words to spell from their letters. Some sample hints and sentences you might give for a Making Words lesson are listed below. This example is for Lesson 30, which has two secret words. Have the child use the letter cards to make the words, then help him or her write the words on the lesson sheet as you work through the lesson. You might say:

   - Use 3 letters to spell **see**. (I can **see** you.)
   - Add 1 letter to spell **seed**. (The plant grew from a tiny **seed**.)
   - Use 4 letters to spell **tree**. (We sat under a big **tree**.)
   - Use 4 letters and spell **rest**. (When we finish, we will take a **rest**.)
   - Use 4 letters and spell **deer**. (The **deer** ran across the road.)
   - Use 5 letters and spell **steer**. (You have to learn to **steer** your bike.)
   - There are two secret words today, and they are both hard ones. (Give the child a minute and then give sentence clues for the two words.) After we worked, we **rested**. We hiked in the **desert**.

3. Using the words made as reference, help the child to complete the sort section of the worksheet by adding the correct beginning letter(s) to the spelling patterns. If the pattern is a word, that word is provided. Read the rhyming words together.

4. Help the child read the sentences listed at the bottom of the lesson sheet and use the rhyming pattern(s) to spell a new word that makes sense in each sentence.

✂ —

Words for Lessons 26-30

(The / indicates words that can be made with the same letters.)

Lesson 26 at sat set bet beat seat/east **beast**
Lesson 27 at act/cat hat heat each **teach/cheat** (2 secret words)
Lesson 28 he cap ape cape each heap **peach/cheap** (2 secret words)
Lesson 29 see tree rest pest seep steep Peter **pester**
Lesson 30 see seed tree rest deer steer **rested/desert** (2 secret words)

Dear Making Words Helper,

Making Words is an activity which helps children become good spellers and word decoders. The attached Making Words lesson is like a puzzle for students to solve with your help. Children enjoy cutting out the letters and arranging them to see that by changing just one letter, adding one letter, or moving the letters around, they have a whole new word. Children also enjoy the puzzle of figuring out the secret word which can be made from all the letters in the activity. (Hide the bottom section of this sheet so that you can keep the **bolded** secret words a secret!)

Your child does Making Words lessons in class, so he or she should be familiar with the steps of making the words, sorting them into rhyming patterns (such as all the words that end in **an**, **ash**, etc.), and then reading and spelling some different words that use the same rhyming patterns. Here are the steps that are needed for each lesson:

1. Help the child write the capital letters on the backs of the letter cards (if they did not complete this while in class), and then cut the letters apart.
2. Use the word list below to identify the words for each lesson. You will need to tell the child what words to spell from their letters. Some sample hints and sentences you might give for a Making Words lesson are listed below. This example is for Lesson 31. Have the child use the letter cards to make the words, then help him or her write the words on the lesson sheet as you work through the lesson. You might say:

- Use 2 letters to spell **it**. (I didn't do **it**.)
- Add 1 letter to spell **pit**. (A peach has a big seed called a **pit**.)
- Move the letters around to spell **tip**. (We left a **tip** for the waitress.)
- Change the first letter and spell **rip**. (I feel and got a **rip** in my pants.)
- Add 1 letter and change **rip** to **ripe**. (The peach is **ripe** enough to eat.)
- Use 4 letters and spell **trip**. (We went on a long **trip**.)
- Add a letter to **trip** and spell **strip**. (Write your name on that **strip** of paper.)
- Leave the letters in **strip** where they are and add the **e** to spell the secret word. (Give the child a minute and then give a sentence clue.) They painted a yellow **stripe** down the middle of the road.

3. Using the words made as reference, help the child to complete the sort section of the worksheet by adding the correct beginning letter(s) to the spelling patterns. If the pattern is a word, that word is provided. Read the rhyming words together.
4. Help the child read the sentences listed at the bottom of the lesson sheet and use the rhyming pattern(s) to spell a new word that makes sense in each sentence.

✂ —

Words for Lessons 31-35

(The / indicates words that can be made with the same letters.)

Lesson 31	it pit/tip rip ripe trip strip **stripe**
Lesson 32	Ed red rid ride side dive dives **drives**
Lesson 33	is sip zip rip ripe size prize **prizes**
Lesson 34	it hit bit big rig birth right **bright**
Lesson 35	if it fit hit lit fight light **flight**

Dear Making Words Helper,

Making Words is an activity which helps children become good spellers and word decoders. The attached Making Words lesson is like a puzzle for students to solve with your help. Children enjoy cutting out the letters and arranging them to see that by changing just one letter, adding one letter, or moving the letters around, they have a whole new word. Children also enjoy the puzzle of figuring out the secret word which can be made from all the letters in the activity. (Hide the bottom section of this sheet so that you can keep the **bolded** secret words a secret!)

Your child does Making Words lessons in class, so he or she should be familiar with the steps of making the words, sorting them into rhyming patterns (such as all the words that end in **an**, **ash**, etc.), and then reading and spelling some different words that use the same rhyming patterns. Here are the steps that are needed for each lesson:

1. Help the child write the capital letters on the backs of the letter cards (if they did not complete this while in class), and then cut the letters apart.
2. Use the word list below to identify the words for each lesson. You will need to tell the child what words to spell from their letters. Some sample hints and sentences you might give for a Making Words lesson are listed below. This example is for Lesson 37, which has two secret words. Have the child use the letter cards to make the words, then help him or her write the words on the lesson sheet as you work through the lesson. You might say:
   *   Use 2 letters to spell **at**. (I stayed **at** my friend's house.)
   *   Add 1 letter to spell **cat**. (A **cat** likes to chase things.)
   *   Change the vowel to spell **cot**. (I slept on the **cot**.)
   *   Add a letter to spell **cost**. (We don't buy expensive clothes because they **cost** too much.)
   *   Use 4 letters to spell **coat**. (She wore a red **coat**.)
   *   There are two secret words today. Leave the letters in **coat** where they are and add the **s** in two different places to spell two words. (Give the child a minute and then give sentence clues for the two words.) I have two **coats**. The land along the ocean is called the **coast**.
3. Using the words made as reference, help the child to complete the sort section of the worksheet by adding the correct beginning letter(s) to the spelling patterns. If the pattern is a word, that word is provided. Read the rhyming words together.
4. Help the child read the sentences listed at the bottom of the lesson sheet and use the rhyming pattern(s) to spell a new word that makes sense in each sentence.

✂ — ✂ — — — — — — —

Words for Lessons 36-40

(The / indicates words that can be made with the same letters.)

Lesson 36   of at oat sat fat flat float **floats**
Lesson 37   at cat cot cost oats coat **coats/coast** (2 secret words)
Lesson 38   no set net not note/tone **stone/notes** (2 secret words)
Lesson 39   us use/Sue bus/sub cub cube **cubes**
Lesson 40   up us Gus our sour soup group **groups**

Dear Making Words Helper,

Making Words is an activity which helps children become good spellers and word decoders. The attached Making Words lesson is like a puzzle for students to solve with your help. Children enjoy cutting out the letters and arranging them to see that by changing just one letter, adding one letter, or moving the letters around, they have a whole new word. Children also enjoy the puzzle of figuring out the secret word which can be made from all the letters in the activity. (Hide the bottom section of this sheet so that you can keep the **bolded** secret words a secret!)

Your child does Making Words lessons in class, so he or she should be familiar with the steps of making the words, sorting them into rhyming patterns (such as all the words that end in **an**, **ash**, etc.), and then reading and spelling some different words that use the same rhyming patterns. Here are the steps that are needed for each lesson:

1. Help the child write the capital letters on the backs of the letter cards (if they did not complete this while in class), and then cut the letters apart.
2. Use the word list below to identify the words for each lesson. You will need to tell the child what words to spell from their letters. Some sample hints and sentences you might give for a Making Words lesson are listed below. This example is for Lesson 41, which has two secret words. Have the child use the letter cards to make the words, then help him or her write the words on the lesson sheet as you work through the lesson. You might say:
   - Use 2 letters to spell **us**. (The man gave **us** cookies.)
   - Use 3 letters to spell **out**. (The dog wants to go **out**.)
   - Use 3 letters to spell **hot**. (It is very **hot** today.)
   - Change the vowel and spell **hut**. (We hid in the old **hut**.)
   - Add 1 letter and spell **shut**. (Please keep the door **shut**.)
   - Change the vowel and spell **shot**. (I took my dog for his rabies **shot**.)
   - There are two secret words today. Leave the letters in **shot** where they are and add the **u** to spell one of them. The other one is harder. (Give the child a minute and then give sentence clues for the two words.) Do not **shout** in the house. We drove **south** to visit our relatives.
3. Using the words made as reference, help the child to complete the sort section of the worksheet by adding the correct beginning letter(s) to the spelling patterns. If the pattern is a word, that word is provided. Read the rhyming words together.
4. Help the child read the sentences listed at the bottom of the lesson sheet and use the rhyming pattern(s) to spell a new word that makes sense in each sentence.

✂ —

Words for Lessons 41-45

(The / indicates words that can be made with the same letters.)

Lesson 41 us out hot hut shut shot **shout/south** (2 secret words)
Lesson 42 or row low/owl owls/slow grow **growls**
Lesson 43 on in win now wow down wind **window**
Lesson 44 Rob mob moo boo boom room broom **brooms**
Lesson 45 so sob rob rot root boot boots **robots**

Dear Making Words Helper,

Making Words is an activity which helps children become good spellers and word decoders. The attached Making Words lesson is like a puzzle for students to solve with your help. Children enjoy cutting out the letters and arranging them to see that by changing just one letter, adding one letter, or moving the letters around, they have a whole new word. Children also enjoy the puzzle of figuring out the secret word which can be made from all the letters in the activity. (Hide the bottom section of this sheet so that you can keep the **bolded** secret words a secret!)

Your child does Making Words lessons in class, so he or she should be familiar with the steps of making the words, sorting them into rhyming patterns (such as all the words that end in **an**, **ash**, etc.), and then reading and spelling some different words that use the same rhyming patterns. Here are the steps that are needed for each lesson:

1. Help the child write the capital letters on the backs of the letter cards (if they did not complete this while in class), and then cut the letters apart.

2. Use the word list below to identify the words for each lesson. You will need to tell the child what words to spell from their letters. Some sample hints and sentences you might give for a Making Words lesson are listed below. This example is for Lesson 46. Have the child use the letter cards to make the words, then help him or her write the words on the lesson sheet as you work through the lesson. You might say:

   - Use 2 letters to spell **at**. (Be ready **at** 7:00.)
   - Add 1 letter to spell **art**. (Sometimes we paint in **art** class.)
   - Use 3 letters to spell **try**. (We **try** to do our very best.)
   - Change the first letter and spell **pry**. (Sometimes it is hard to **pry** something open.)
   - Add 1 letter to **pry** to spell **pray**. (We **pray** it won't rain on Saturday.)
   - Change 1 letter and spell **tray**. (He knocked over the **tray**.)
   - Use 4 letters and spell **part**. (Which **part** of the story did you like best?)
   - Keep the letters in **part** and add the **y** someplace and you will have the secret word. (Give the child a minute and then give a sentence clue.) It was a great **party**.

3. Using the words made as reference, help the child to complete the sort section of the worksheet by adding the correct beginning letter(s) to the spelling patterns. If the pattern is a word, that word is provided. Read the rhyming words together.

4. Help the child read the sentences listed at the bottom of the lesson sheet and use the rhyming pattern(s) to spell a new word that makes sense in each sentence.

✂--

Words for Lessons 46-50

(The / indicates words that can be made with the same letters.)

Lesson 46	at art try pry pray tray part **party**
Lesson 47	or for toy Roy try fry fort **forty**
Lesson 48	it pit/tip lip lot pot plot **pilot**
Lesson 49	lip lie pie like lick pick clip **pickle**
Lesson 50	it lit kit kite like lick tick **tickle**

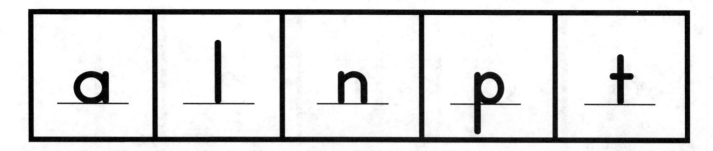

Name_____ Lesson 1

1. Make Words

— — —

— — —

___ ___ ___ ___

___ ___ ___

___ ___ ___

___ ___ ___

___ ___ ___ ___ ___

___ ___ ___ ___ ___ ___

2. Sort

at   an

__at   __an

                  __an

                  ___ ___an

_____

3. Transfer

1. I have a black c_____.

2. We r_____ home.

a	c	h	n	t

Name_____

1. Make Words

___ ___

___ ___

___ ___ ___

___ ___ ___

___ ___ ___

___ ___ ___

___ ___ ___ ___

2. Sort

at   an

__at   __an

            __an

__ __an

ant

__ __ant

3. Transfer

1. The p_____ is hot.

2. I like to ride in a v_____.

a	h	m	s	s

Name_____

1. Make Words

___ ___ ___

___ ___ ___

___ ___ ___ ___

___ ___ ___ ___

___ ___ ___ ___

___ ___ ___ ___ ___

___ ___ ___ ___ ___ ___

2. Sort

as   am

___as   ___am

___am

ash

___ash

___ ___ash

3. Transfer

1. Do you like j_____?

2. The car was in a cr_____.

a	c	k	n	s

Name_____   Lesson 4

1. Make Words

___ ___

___ ___

___ ___ ___

___ ___ ___

___ ___ ___ ___

___ ___ ___ ___

___ ___ ___ ___

2. Sort

an

___an

___ ___an

___ack

___ ___ack

3. Transfer

1. Do you like to run on the tr_____?

2. My dog is a t_____ color.

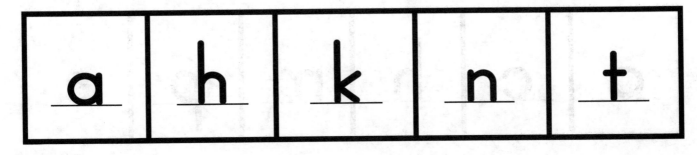

Name_____   **Lesson 5**

1. Make Words

___ ___

___ ___

___ ___ ___

___ ___ ___

___ ___ ___

___ ___ ___

___ ___ ___ ___

2. Sort

at   an

___at   ___an

___ank

___ank

___ank

___ ___ank

3. Transfer

1. My cat is f_____.
2. We went to the b_____.

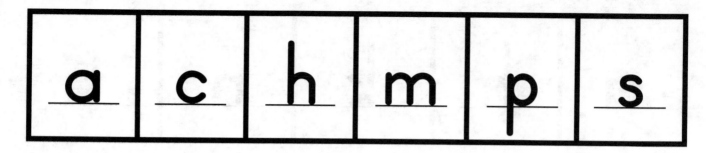

Name_____   Lesson 6

1. Make Words

___ ___ ___

___ ___ ___

___ ___ ___

___ ___ ___

___ ___ ___

___ ___ ___ ___

___ ___ ___ ___

2. Sort

___am   ___ap

___am   ___ap

___am

___amp

___ ___amp

3. Transfer

1. Do not sl_____ the door!

2. We cl_____ our hands.

a	h	k	r	s	s

Name_____   **Lesson 7**

1. Make Words

___ ___

___ ___ ___

___ ___ ___

___ ___ ___

___ ___ ___

___ ___ ___ ___

___ ___ ___ ___ ___

___ ___ ___ ___ ___

2. Sort

as   ash

___as   ___ash

ark

___ ___ ___ark

3. Transfer

1. It is d_____ at night.

2. Put that in the tr_____.

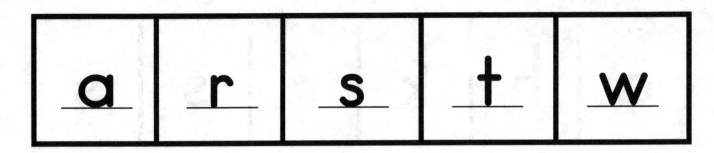

Name_____

1. Make Words

_____

_____

_____

_____

_____

_____

2. Sort

at

__at

__at

__aw

__aw

__ __ __aw

3. Transfer

1. In school, I like to dr_____.

2. I wear a h_____ in the sun.

22

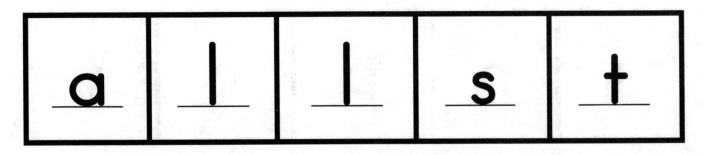

Name_____ **Lesson 9**

1. Make Words

___ ___ ___

___ ___ ___

___ ___ ___ ___

___ ___ ___ ___ ___

___ ___ ___ ___ ___

___ ___ ___ ___ ___

2. Sort

at

__at

all

__all

__ __all

3. Transfer

1. We had a fl_____ tire.

2. I will c_____ my mother.

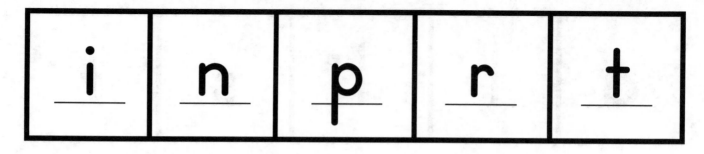

Name_____ **Lesson 10**

1. Make Words

___ ___

___ ___

___ ___ ___

___ ___ ___

___ ___ ___

___ ___ ___

___ ___ ___ ___

___ ___ ___ ___ ___

2. Sort

in   it

___in   ___it

___ip

___ip

___ ___ip

3. Transfer

1. He can sk_____.

2. I s_____ in my chair.

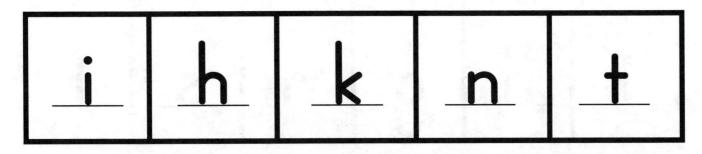

Name_____   Lesson 11

1. Make Words

___ ___

___ ___

___ ___ ___

___ ___ ___

___ ___ ___

___ ___ ___ ___

___ ___ ___ — ___

2. Sort

in   it

__in   __it

___ ___in   ___it

ink

__ink

__ __ink

3. Transfer

1. The cat sp_____ at the dog.

2. I like the color p_____.

25   © Carson-Dellosa CD-2608

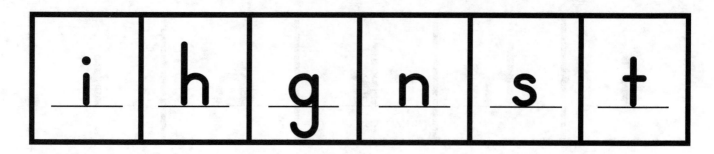

| i | h | g | n | s | t |

Name_____

1. Make Words

___ ___ ___

___ ___ ___

___ ___ ___ ___

___ ___ ___ ___

___ ___ ___ ___

___ ___ ___ ___ ___

___ ___ ___ ___ ___ ___

2. Sort

in   it

___in   ___it

            ___it

___ing

___ ___ing

3. Transfer

1. The dog b_____ the cat.

2. I bumped my ch_____.

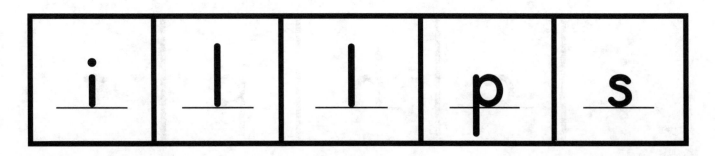

i	l	l	p	s

Name_____   **Lesson 13**

1. Make Words

___ ___

___ ___ ___

___ ___ ___

___ ___ ___ ___

___ ___ ___ ___

___ ___ ___ ___

___ ___ ___ ___

2. Sort

___ip

___ip

___ ___ip

___ill

___ ___ill

3. Transfer

1. The house is on a h_____.

2. We went on a tr_____.

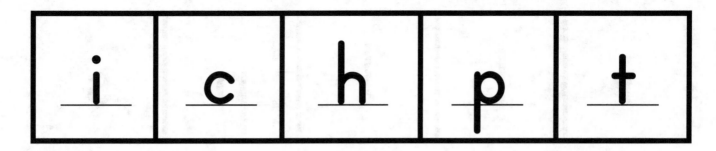

i	c	h	p	t

Name_____   **Lesson 14**

1. Make Words

___ ___

___ ___

___ ___ ___

___ ___ ___

___ ___ ___ ___

___ ___ ___ ___

___ ___ ___ ___ ___

2. Sort

___ip   it

___ ___ip   ___it

               ___it

itch

___itch

3. Transfer

1. Turn on the light sw_____.

2. I need a paper cl_____.

e	b	d	n	s

Name_____ Lesson 15

1. Make Words

__ __

__ __ __

__ __ __

__ __ __ __

__ __ __ __

__ __ __ __

__ __ __ __ __

2. Sort

Ed   end

__ed   __end

__ed   __end

ends

__ends

3. Transfer

1. I like the color r_____.

2. Did you sp_____ the money?

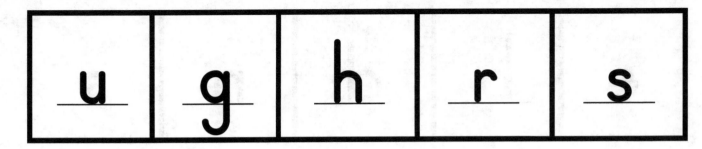

Name_____ **Lesson 16**

1. Make Words

_ _ _ _

_ _ _ _ _

_ _ _ _

_ _ _ _ _

_ _ _ _ _

_ _ _ _ _

_ _ _ _ _ _

2. Sort

___ush   ___ugs

___ush   ___ugs

___ug

___ug

_ _ _ ___ug

3. Transfer

1. I saw a b_____ on the rug.

2. Br_____ your teeth.

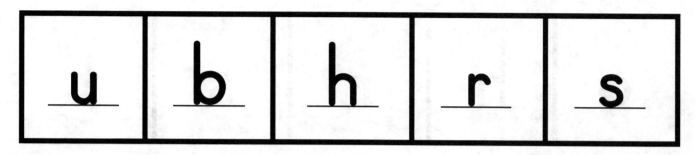

Name_____   **Lesson 17**

1. Make Words

___ ___ ___

___ ___ ___

___ ___ ___

___ ___ ___

___ ___ ___

___ ___ ___ ___

___ ___ ___ ___

2. Sort

us   ___ush

___us   ___ ___ush

___ub

___ub

___ub

___ ___ ___ub

3. Transfer

1. Wash the dog in the t_____.

2. I will scr_____ the pan.

o	h	r	s	t

Name_____ **Lesson 18**

1. Make Words

___ ___ ___

___ ___ ___

___ ___ ___ ___

___ ___ ___ ___

___ ___ ___ ___

___ ___ ___ ___

___ ___ ___ ___

2. Sort

___ ___ot

___ ___ot

___ ___ ___ot

___ ___ort

___ ___ ___ort

3. Transfer

1. What is your favorite sp_____?
2. My shirt has a sp_____ on it.

a	i	b	n	r

Name_____

1. Make Words

___ ___

___ ___

___ ___ ___

___ ___ ___

___ ___ ___ ___

___ ___ ___ ___

___ ___ ___ ___ ___

2. Sort

an

___an

___an

___ ___ ___an

___ain

___ ___ ___ain

3. Transfer

1. His name is D_____.

2. We rode on the tr_____.

a	i	n	r	t

Name_____ **Lesson 20**

1. Make Words

___ ___ ___

___ ___ ___

___ ___ ___ ___

___ ___ ___ ___

___ ___ ___ ___

___ ___ ___ ___ ___

___ ___ ___ ___ ___ ___

2. Sort

at   an

__at   __an

__an

__ain

__ ___ain

3. Transfer

1. I fed my c_____.

2. I think with my br_____.

a	e	k	s	t

1. Make Words

___ ___ ___

___ ___ ___ ___

___ ___ ___ ___

___ ___ ___ ___

___ ___ ___ ___

___ ___ ___ ___ ___

___ ___ ___ ___ ___

___ ___ ___ ___ ___ ___

2. Sort

at   eat

__at   __eat

                ate

                __ate

                __ __ate

3. Transfer

1. What is the d_____ today?

2. I like wh_____ bread.

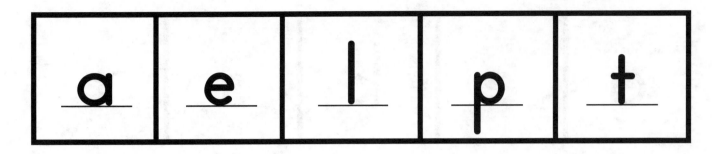

Name_____ Lesson 22

1. Make Words

___ ___

___ ___ ___

___ ___ ___

___ ___ ___

___ ___ ___

___ ___ ___ ___

___ ___ ___ ___

2. Sort

at   ___et

___at   ___et

ate

___ate

___ ___ate

3. Transfer

1. We took the dog to the v_____.

2. He is l_____.

36   © Carson-Dellosa CD-2608

a	r	s	t	y

Name_____   **Lesson 23**

1. Make Words

__ __ __

__ __ __ __

__ __ __ __

__ __ __ __

__ __ __ __ __

__ __ __ __ __ __

__ __ __ __ __

2. Sort

at

__at

__at

__ay

__ay

__ __ay

__ __ __ay

3. Transfer

1. I like to play with cl_____.

2. I like the month of M_____.

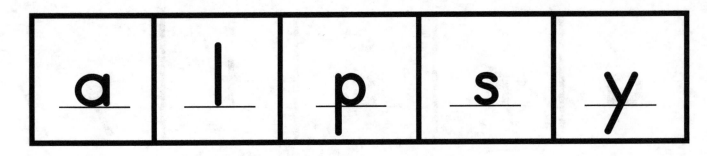

a	l	p	s	y

Name_____ **Lesson 24**

1. Make Words

___ ___

___ ___ ___

___ ___ ___

___ ___ ___

___ ___ ___

___ ___ ___

___ ___ ___ ___

___ ___ ___ ___ ___

2. Sort

Al   __ap

__al   __ap

__ay

__ay

__ __ __ay

3. Transfer

1. I put the milk on my tr_____.

2. We will cl_____ at the end.

a	e	m	s	t

Name_____   **Lesson 25**

1. Make Words

___ ___

___ ___ ___

___ ___ ___

___ ___ ___ ___

___ ___ ___ ___

___ ___ ___ ___

___ ___ ___ ___ ___ ___

___ ___ ___ ___ ___

2. Sort

___et   ___eat

___et   ___eat

___eam

___ ___eam

3. Transfer

1. I gave my cat a tr_____.

2. Do not scr_____!

a	e	b	s	t

Name_____ **Lesson 26**

1. Make Words

___ ___ ___

___ ___ ___

___ ___ ___

___ ___ ___

___ ___ ___ ___

___ ___ ___ ___

___ ___ ___ ___

2. Sort

at   ___et

___at   ___et

___eat   east

___eat   ___east

3. Transfer

1. It is not fair to ch_____.

2. On Thanksgiving, we had a f_____.

a	e	c	h	t

1. Make Words

___ ___

___ ___ ___

___ ___ ___

___ ___ ___

___ ___ ___ ___

___ ___ ___ ___

___ ___ ___ ___

2. Sort

at   ___eat

___at   ___ ___ ___eat

___at

each

___each

3. Transfer

1. The cat ran after the r_____.

2. A p_____ is a fruit.

a	e	c	h	p

Name_____ Lesson 28

1. Make Words

___ ___

___ ___ ___

___ ___ ___ ___

___ ___ ___ ___

___ ___ ___ ___ ___

___ ___ ___ ___ ___

___ ___ ___ ___ ___

2. Sort

ape   each

__ape   ___each

___eap

___ ___eap

3. Transfer

1. I have fun at the b_____.

2. Do you like gr_____ juice?

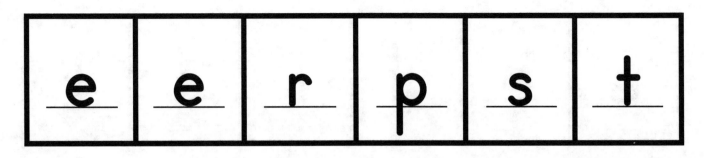

Name_____ **Lesson 29**

1. Make Words

___ ___ ___

___ ___ ___ ___

___ ___ ___ ___

___ ___ ___ ___

___ ___ ___ ___

___ ___ ___ ___ ___

___ ___ ___ ___ ___

___ ___ ___ ___ ___ ___

2. Sort

___ee   ___est

___ ___ee   ___est

___eep

___ ___eep

3. Transfer

1. We will go w_____.

2. The horn went b_____.

e	e	d	r	s	t

Name_____   **Lesson 30**

1. Make Words | **2. Sort**

___ ___ ___ ___

___ ___ ___ ___ ___

___ ___ ___ ___ ___   ___ee

___ ___ ___ ___ ___   ___ ___ee

___ ___ ___ ___ ___

___ ___ ___ ___ ___ ___   ___eer

___ ___ ___ ___ ___ ___ ___   ___ ___eer

3. Transfer

1. A b_____ can sting.

2. Which team will you ch_____ for?

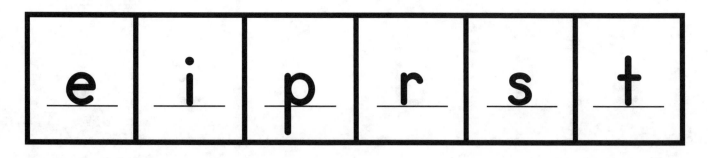

| e | i | p | r | s | t |

Name_____   **Lesson 31**

1. Make Words

___ ___

___ ___ ___

___ ___ ___

___ ___ ___

___ ___ ___ ___

___ ___ ___ ___

___ ___ ___ ___ ___

___ ___ ___ ___ ___ ___

2. Sort

it

___it

___ip

___ip

___ ___ip

___ ___ ___ip

___ipe

___ ___ ___ipe

3. Transfer

1. Do not sl_____ and fall.

2. I will w_____ up the mess.

e	i	d	r	s	v

Name_____   **Lesson 32**

1. Make Words

___ ___ ___

___ ___ ___ ___

___ ___ ___ ___

___ ___ ___ ___ ___

___ ___ ___ ___ ___

___ ___ ___ ___ ___ ___

___ ___ ___ ___ ___ ___ ___

2. Sort

Ed   __ide

__ed   __ide

            __ives

            __ives

3. Transfer

1. I sleep in my b_____.
2. We played h_____ and seek.

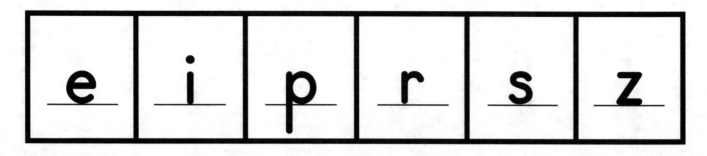

| e | i | p | r | s | z |

Name_____ **Lesson 33**

1. Make Words

___ ___ ___

___ ___ ___

___ ___ ___

___ ___ ___

___ ___ ___ ___

___ ___ ___ ___

___ ___ ___ ___ ___

2. Sort

___ip

___ip

___ip

___ize

___ ___ize

3. Transfer

1. We went on a long tr_____.

2. We went on a big sh_____.

i	b	g	h	r	t

Name_____ Lesson 34

1. Make Words

___ ___ ___

___ ___ ___

___ ___ ___

___ ___ ___

___ ___ ___ ___

___ ___ ___ ___

___ ___ ___ ___

2. Sort

it   __ig

__it   __ig

__it

__ight

__ __ight

3. Transfer

1. We go to sleep at n_____.

2. I like to d_____ in the sand.

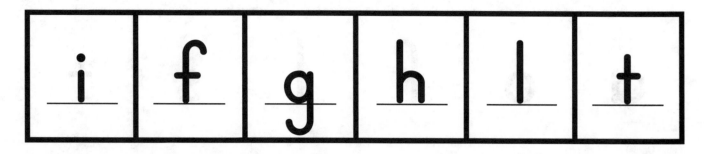

| i | f | g | h | l | t |

Name_____ **Lesson 35**

1. Make Words

___ ___

___ ___

___ ___ ___

___ ___ ___

___ ___ ___ ___

___ ___ ___ ___

___ ___ ___ ___ ___

2. Sort

it

___it

___it

___it

___ight

___ight

___ ___ight

3. Transfer

1. I s_____ in my seat.

2. The sun is br_____.

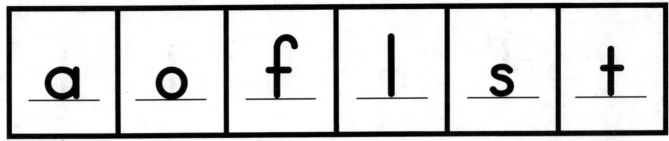

(Letter Cards)

Name_____ **Lesson 36**

1. Make Words

___ ___

___ ___ ___

___ ___ ___ ___

___ ___ ___ ___

___ ___ ___ ___

___ ___ ___ ___ ___

___ ___ ___ ___ ___ ___

___ ___ ___ ___ ___ ___ ___

2. Sort

at

___at

___at

___at

___ ___ ___at

oat

___ ___ ___oat

3. Transfer

1. We went for a b_____ ride.

2. Hit the ball with the b_____.

a	o	c	s	t

Name_____   Lesson 37

1. Make Words   **2. Sort**

___ ___

___ ___ ___

___ ___ ___

___ ___ ___ ___

___ ___ ___ ___

___ ___ ___ ___

___ ___ ___ ___ ___

___ ___ ___ ___

at

___at

oats

___oats

3. Transfer

1. Put on your h_____.

2. The boat fl_____ in the water.

e	o	n	s	t

Name_____ **Lesson 38**

1. Make Words

___ ___

___ ___ ___

___ ___ ___

___ ___ ___

___ ___ ___ ___

___ ___ ___ ___

___ ___ ___ ___ ___

___ ___ ___ ___

2. Sort

___et

___et

___one

___ ___one

3. Transfer

1. Did you get w_____?

2. The dog has a b_____.

e	u	b	c	s

Name_____   **Lesson 39**

1. Make Words

__ __

__ __ __

__ __ __

__ __ __

__ __ __

__ __ __ __

__ __ __ __ __

2. Sort

us

___us

___ub

___ub

3. Transfer

1. Can I be in your cl_____?

2. The man's name is G_____.

o	u	g	p	r	s

Name_____   **Lesson 40**

1. Make Words

___ ___

___ ___

___ ___ ___

___ ___ ___

___ ___ ___ ___

___ ___ ___ ___ ___

___ ___ ___ ___ ___ ___

2. Sort

us   our

___us   ___our

___oup

___ ___oup

3. Transfer

1. We make bread with fl_____.

2. We ride to school on the b_____.

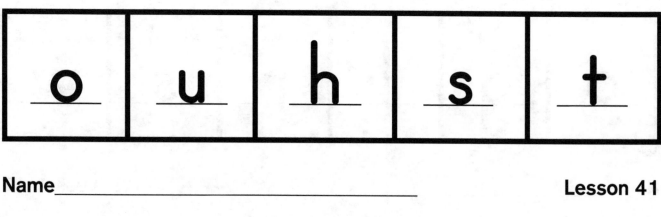

Name_____   **Lesson 41**

1. Make Words

___ ___

___ ___ ___

___ ___ ___

___ ___ ___

___ ___ ___ ___

___ ___ ___ ___

___ ___ ___ ___

2. Sort

out

___ ___out

___ot

___ ___ot

___ut

___ ___ut

3. Transfer

1. I have a c_____ on my finger.

2. She is n_____ here.

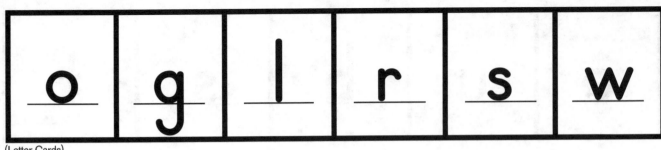

(Letter Cards)

Name_____ **Lesson 42**

1. Make Words

___ ___

___ ___ ___

___ ___ ___

___ ___ ___

___ ___ ___ ___

___ ___ ___ ___

___ ___ ___ ___

___ ___ ___ ___ ___

2. Sort

___OW

___OW

___ ___OW

___ ___OW

owls

___ ___owls

3. Transfer

1. I will bl_____ up the balloon.

2. The wolf h_____ at the moon.

56

i	o	d	n	w	w

1. Make Words

___ ___

___ ___

___ ___ ___

___ ___ ___

___ ___ ___

___ ___ ___ ___

___ ___ ___ ___

___ ___ ___ ___ ___

2. Sort

in

___in

___ow

___ow

3. Transfer

1. He has a tw_____ brother.

2. I don't know h_____ to do that.

o	o	b	m	r	s

(Letter Cards)

Name_____ **Lesson 44**

1. Make Words

___ ___ ___

___ ___ ___

___ ___ ___

___ ___ ___

___ ___ ___ ___

___ ___ ___ ___

___ ___ ___ ___ ___

___ ___ ___ ___ ___

2. Sort

___ob   ___oo

___ob   ___oo

___oom

___oom

___ ___oom

3. Transfer

1. I like corn on the c_____.

2. A jet can z_____.

o	o	b	r	s	t

Name_____

1. Make Words

___ ___

___ ___ ___

___ ___ ___

___ ___ ___

___ ___ ___ ___

___ ___ ___ ___

___ ___ ___ ___ ___

2. Sort

___ob

___ob

___oot

___oot

3. Transfer

1. B_____ is my brother.

2. You did a good j_____.

a	p	r	t	y

Name_____

1. Make Words

___ ___

___ ___ ___

___ ___ ___

___ ___ ___ ___

___ ___ ___ ___

___ ___ ___ ___ ___

2. Sort

art   ___ ___y

___art   ___ ___y

___ ___ay

___ ___ay

3. Transfer

1. I can read the ch_____.

2. I like to play with cl_____.

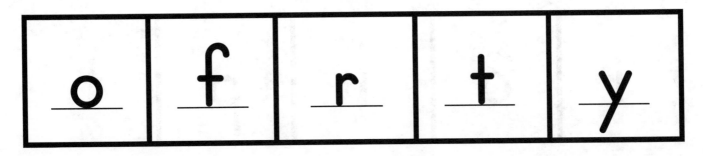

Name_____   **Lesson 47**

1. Make Words

____ ____ ____

____ ____ ____ ____

____ ____ ____ ____

____ ____ ____ ____

____ ____ ____ ____

____ ____ ____ ____ ____

2. Sort

____oy   or

____oy   ____or

____ ____y

____ ____y

_____

3. Transfer

1. Roy is a b_____.

2. Do not cr_____.

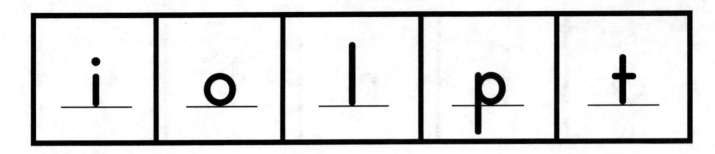

Name_____ **Lesson 48**

1. Make Words

___ ___ ___

___ ___ ___ ___

___ ___ ___ ___

___ ___ ___ ___

___ ___ ___ ___

___ ___ ___ ___

___ ___ ___ ___ ___

___ ___ ___ ___ ___

2. Sort

it   ___ip

___it   ___ip

___ot

___ot

___ ___ot

3. Transfer

1. I can do a fl_____.

2. The doctor gave me a sh_____.

e	i	c	k	l	p

Name_____ **Lesson 49**

1. Make Words

_____ _____ _____ _____

_____ _____ _____

_____ _____ _____

_____ _____ _____ _____ _____

_____ _____ _____ _____ _____

_____ _____ _____ _____

_____ _____ _____

_____ _____ _____ _____ _____ _____

2. Sort

___ick   ___ie

___ick   ___ie

          ___ip

___ ___ip

3. Transfer

1. Can you sk_____?

2. The man did a magic tr_____.

e	i	c	k	l	t

(Letter Cards)

Name_____   **Lesson 50**

1. Make Words

___ ___

___ ___ ___

___ ___ ___

___ ___ ___ ___

___ ___ ___ ___

___ ___ ___ ___

___ ___ ___ ___ ___

2. Sort

it

__it

__it

__ick

__ick

3. Transfer

1. That coat does not f_____.

2. You can p_____ the one you want.